MW01615185

True Success and How to Attain It

Man's Greatest Need

Dr. Wayne Mack

Calvary Press
PO Box 805
Amityville, NY 11701
www.calvarypress.com

Calvary Press
PO Box 805
Amityville, NY 11701
USA
1-800-789-8175
www.calvarypress.com
e-mail: calvrypres@aol.com

ISBN 1-879737-53-1

2004 Calvary Press

Cover and Page Design by: Advantage Color Inc., Copiague, New York

Dr. Wayne Mack
        True Success and How to Attain It.
        Man's Greatest Need.

Recommended Dewey Decimal Classification: 234

Suggested Subject Headings

1. Religion-Church Life-Ministry
2. Christian Literature-Inspirational
3. Ministry-Teaching Literature
I. Title

Manufactured in the United States of America
1 2 3 4 5 6 7 8 9 10   99 00 01

True Success
and
How to Attain It

HAVE YOU EVER PLANNED TO FAIL?

Have you ever met someone who claimed, "My goal in life is to be a failure"? In my lifetime, I have talked to and counseled thousands of people. I have never talked to a young person who said that they looked forward to a life of failure. Likewise, I have never spoken with an older person who looked back on their life and said that they were glad it was a failure. Everyone wants to be a success in some measure.

Our Creator wants us to be a success as well. I believe that God makes it clear in His Word that He wants His children to have ambition. In fact, when God describes believers, one of the ways in which He does it is as "over-comers," and over-comers are winners.

Romans 8:37 says, "But in all these things we *overwhelmingly conquer* through Him who loved us." Indeed, II Corinthians 2:14 teaches, "But thanks be to God, who always leads us in *triumph* in Christ..."

These are strong words—"overwhelmingly conquer" and "triumph," and they imply that we do far more than just "squeak by" as believers. In I John 5:4 the Bible says, "For whatever is born of God *overcomes* the world…" Christians are winners!

In Revelation 2 and 3, we find the seven letters to the seven churches in Asia Minor. In every letter, the Lord speaks of those who overcome: "to him who overcomes," or "he who overcomes." Our Lord uses these two phrases to describe believers because a Christian is one who overcomes. In fact, Christ's message to the churches in these letters was that if we do not overcome in the end, we are not true believers.

THE PROBLEM WITH SUCCESS

So then, if God wants us to be successful, what is wrong with wanting success? The problem with us wanting success is not that all success is wrong, but that success *the world's way* is wrong. More specifically, there are three common problems that hinder our pursuit of the right kind of success.

The first problem is that, in many cases, we have wrongly defined what it means to be successful. Our idea of success is not God's idea of success; it is the world's idea. The second problem is that we often desire success for the wrong reasons. The third problem is that we often go about trying to achieve success in the wrong way.

I Timothy 4:7-10 is a passage that provides valuable insight into these three problems because it teaches us what it means to be truly successful, why we should desire it, and how we should achieve it. The apostle Paul, writing by the inspiration of the Holy Spirit, wrote:

But have nothing to do with worldly fables fit only for old women. On the other hand, *discipline yourself for the purpose of godliness;* for bodily discipline is only a little profit, but *godliness is profitable for all things, since it holds promise for the present life and also for the life to come.* It is a trustworthy statement deserving full acceptance. *For it is for this we labor and strive,* because we have fixed our hope on the living God, who is the Savior of all men, especially of believers.

In verse seven, Paul said that we are to discipline ourselves for the purpose of godliness. Another translation of this phrase could be "orient yourself towards" godliness. In other words, godliness is to be the aim of our lives, our ultimate goal, our sole purpose and object. He emphasized this concept again in verse ten when he wrote, "*It is for this* we labor and strive." Another translation of this phrase is "*It is for this goal* we labor and strive." Our goal in life, as believers, is godliness. True success, as far as God is concerned, is for us to be godly men and women.

As we study this text further, I want us to ask and answer three questions. First, why is true success equated with godliness? Second, what is godliness? Third, how is godliness to be attained? The answers to these three questions will not only equip us to be truly successful believers, but will make firm in our minds why godliness is to be our ultimate goal in life.

Application Questions:

1. The pursuit of which type of success, God's or the world's, would you say has most characterized your life so far?

2. What is wrong with wanting and pursuing the wrong kind of success?

3. What is one aspect of the world's definition of success that has influenced you in the past?

GODLINESS IS PROFITABLE
FOR ALL THINGS

In verse seven, Paul wrote, "…discipline yourself for the purpose of godliness." In verse eight, Paul explained why we must discipline ourselves for godliness: "godliness is *profitable for all things.*" In these two verses we find the answer to our first question. Godliness is equated with true success *because it is beneficial for everything!*

In verse eight, Paul allowed that bodily discipline had some, small value for life. "BUT," he said, "godliness is profitable for *all things.*" While there are any number of other things that Paul could have compared the value of godliness to—a good education, career preparation, or good financial planning, he probably chose bodily discipline because it was a fad at the time in Ephesus. This was where he was ministering when he wrote to Timothy.

Some other things that Paul wrote in this letter to Timothy point to this as well. In the first few verses of chapter four, he wrote about those who prided themselves in their asceticism, or self-denial. Ascetics were very careful to control their bodily appetites. They exercised self-control in the area of food—not eating some foods—and in sexual relations even within marriage. They may have even been into physical exercise as so many are today.

While Paul acknowledged that this kind of self-control had some value, he challenged Timothy with the fact that it was very limited in comparison with the value of godliness. Godliness, according to the Word of God as written by the apostle Paul, is of *unlimited* value. It is profitable in *every way*. However, when we read that godliness is profitable in every way, it is important for us to understand what Paul did *not* mean by the words "in every way."

For example, he was not teaching that godly people would become millionaires. Countless godly people in this world have not been financially wealthy. In fact, many have been quite poor in material ways. Paul himself, a very godly man, said that he knew what it was to get along with humble means, to go hungry, and to suffer need (Phil. 4:12).

His need was certainly not due to a lack of godliness in his life.

Paul was also not teaching that godly people would never encounter problems in life or would be able to escape problems because of their godliness. In II Corinthians 4:8, Paul wrote that he was "afflicted in every way." He went on to describe the nature of his afflictions, and they were evidently quite severe (4:8-11). Again, Paul's abundance of difficulties were not due to his ungodliness.

In light of this, it is apparent that godliness does not guarantee wealth, health, or a free pass on life's problems. In other words, godliness does not mean success on the world's terms. If not that, then what did Paul mean when he said, "godliness is profitable for all things"?

Looking back at I Timothy 4, let's consider what the end of verse eight says: "…since it holds promise *for* the present life and also *for* the life to come." Another translation of this is, "…since it holds promise *of* the present life and *of* the life which is to come."

Using the first translation, with the word "for," Paul may have been referring to the sense of well-being that a godly person experiences. Psalm 112:1 says, "...How *blessed* is the man who fears the Lord..." Godly people are blessed with a sense of great security in the Lord. Proverbs 14:26 teaches, "*In the fear of the Lord there is strong confidence*, and his children will have refuge."

Godly people are also blessed with the knowledge that they have purpose and direction in life. They are aware of the fact that they belong to God and that they have a real relationship with their Creator. Still further, they experience the true contentment that we discussed in chapter one and that Paul says is a great blessing: "But godliness actually is a means of *great gain* when accompanied by contentment" (I Timothy 6:6). All of these things are of great worth to the godly person and, in that sense, are "profitable."

Not only that, but godliness is the purpose of our redemption. We have been saved by God not only to escape eternal punishment and to simply function on earth until we physically die, but also to become more like Christ while we live out the rest of our physical life. As we become more like Christ, we also experience great blessing because we are fulfilling the purpose for which we were created and redeemed.

Considering the second translation, with the word "of," Paul may have been saying that the godly person will experience fullness of life. In the New Testament, there are several Greek words that are translated "life." One is the word *bios* (from which we get the word "biology"); another is the word *psuche*. The Greek word that is used in I Timothy 4:8, is the word *zoe*.

This word *zoe* refers to both the existence of life and the substance, or quality, of life. It is the same word that Jesus used in John 17:3 when He said, "This is eternal life, that they may know You, the only true God, and Jesus Christ whom You have sent." The eternal life that we as believers look forward to is much more than simply living for days on end. Eternal life is abundant life that is lived out in the immediate presence of the living God. Jesus also said, "…I came that they may have life, and have it abundantly" (John 10:10).

In other words, Paul may have been saying that the godly person will learn what it is to live as God originally intended—experiencing both physical and spiritual life—because they know God and God is life, the very principal and essence of it. Indeed, we know that God made us for Himself and intended us to be in fellowship with Him. The person who knows God and is growing daily in godliness will experience more and more fellowship with and knowledge of the living God.

The psalmist wrote, "My flesh and my heart may fail, but God is the strength of my heart and my portion forever" (Psalm 73:26). In that sense, godliness is most certainly "profitable for all things" because there is nothing that is of more value, or of any value, compared to the eternal and immeasurable value of knowing God.

Godliness, therefore, is rightly equated with true success because godliness is beneficial for everything that is worth having: it is a source of great blessing; it is the kind of life that we were created to live; and it is the principal means by which we grow in our relationship with God.

Application Questions:

1. Why is godliness equated with true success?

2. When Paul said that godliness is profitable for all things, what did he <u>not</u> mean?

3. Why are these things not a part of true success?

4. What are some of the benefits of godliness?

5. Write out Psalm 73:26. What does this verse teach about true success?

WHAT GODLINESS IS NOT

The second question that we wish to answer is this: what is godliness? Since, as we just learned, godliness is the means by which we can enjoy true success, then we ought to know what it is. Let's begin exploring what godliness is by first looking at what it is not.

Godliness is *not* merely religious activity. A person can be very busy in the church, teaching Sunday school classes, greeting visitors, serving on committees, but not be godly. Jesus taught this in Matthew 7:22-23 when He said, "Many will say to Me on that day, 'Lord, Lord, did we not prophesy in Your name, and in Your name cast out demons, and in Your name perform many miracles?' And then I will declare to them, 'I never knew you; depart from Me, you who practice lawlessness.'" Indeed, Christ repeatedly rebuked the Pharisees for loving religious activity but not loving God or other people (Matthew 23:23).

Godliness is also *not* simply religious orthodoxy. It is possible to have one's doctrine straight—to believe the Bible and the great truths of the Christian faith—and not be a godly person. James 2:19 says, "You believe that God is one. You do well; the demons also believe, and shudder." It is possible to believe in the virgin birth, the sinless life of Christ, the crucifixion and resurrection (indeed, Satan himself knows all these things to be true), and not be godly.

Further, godliness is *not* just success in Christian work. Throughout history, ungodly people have been used by God to bring others to Christ. Some evangelists, claiming to be godly, have been very successful in ministry, but the rebellion in their hearts was later revealed. In Philippians 1:15-18, Paul mentioned his dealings with some people like this:

> **Some, to be sure, are preaching Christ even from envy and strife, but some also from good will...the former proclaim Christ out of selfish ambition rather than from pure motives...What then? Only that in every way, whether in pretense or in truth, Christ is proclaimed; and in this I rejoice...**

Paul wrote that God was using the gospel preaching of both godly and ungodly people. It is possible, therefore, to be a "success" in ministry from man's perspective and not be successful in personal godliness.

Let it be understood that I am in no way intending to minimize or denigrate any of these activities. It is very good for us to be involved in the ministry of the church, to have our doctrine straight, and to be successful in our ministry for God. We are called to such good works in Christ Jesus, but doing these things does not make us godly.

Application Questions:

1. **Why is religious activity not equal to godliness?**

2. **Why is religious orthodoxy not equal to godliness?**

3. **Why is success in ministry not equal to godliness?**

4. **In what ways have you lived, or are you living, as if any of these three things were equal to godliness?**

EXAMPLES OF GODLINESS

Having considered what godliness is not and having looked at a few examples of ungodly people doing good things, let's consider some examples of people in the Bible who were truly godly. For example, Enoch was a godly man. We know very little about this man from the record of Scripture, but what we know says a great deal. In fact, I often pray, "Oh God, make me like Enoch."

The Bible talks about Enoch's life in two places. Genesis 5:24 says, "Enoch walked with God; and he was not, for God took him." Hebrews 11:5 echoes, "By faith Enoch was taken up so that he would not see death; and he was not found because God took him up; for he obtained the witness that before his being taken up he was pleasing to God."

The testimony about Enoch is that he *walked with God* and *pleased God*. These are the marks of a godly life. A person who *walks* with God has regular fellowship with Him and is constantly in His presence because God is of supreme importance in his life. A person who *pleases* God obeys in all things for the same reason. Everything that Enoch thought, said, and did was directed towards God. That is godliness.

The apostle Paul was a godly man. In Philippians 1:20-21, Paul wrote, "…according to my earnest expectation and hope, that I will not be put to shame in anything, but that with all boldness, Christ will even now, as always, be exalted in my body, whether by life or by death. *For to me, to live is Christ and to die is gain.*" Writing from prison, Paul knew that he might be killed at any moment, yet it did not matter. What mattered to Paul was that Christ received all the glory through his, Paul's, life or death. That is godliness.

The words of the psalmist in Psalm 73 are the words of a godly man. In verses 25-26, he says, "Who have I in heaven but You? And besides You, I desire nothing on earth. My flesh and my heart may fail, but God is the strength of my heart and my portion forever." God was *all* that this man needed or wanted.

Consider the remarkable meaning of his words in these verses. First, God was all that he wanted in heaven. Some people want to go to heaven because they are so afraid of hell. Others want to go to heaven because they have heard about pearly gates and streets of gold. Still others think about those who have gone before them—loved ones that have died, great saints of the faith, people from Bible times—and cannot wait to see them in heaven.

The psalmist's thoughts about heaven were different, however. He had a singular focus: seeing and being with God. To see God "face to face" and to "know fully just as I also have been fully known" were his heart's desire (I Corinthians 13:12). To him, heaven would be hell without God. These are the thoughts and desires of a godly person.

Second, God was all that he wanted on earth. He wrote that he desired "*nothing* on earth" besides God (73:25). What are the things that we desire on earth? What makes us upset not to have? We are often very attached to money, health, a good reputation, approval, praise, our jobs, and countless other things. If any of these things—if *anything*—comes before God, then godliness is lacking in some measure. A godly person desires God above anything in all of heaven and earth.

Our Lord Jesus Christ is, of course, the ultimate example of godliness. In John 4:34, He said, " 'My food is to do the will of Him who sent Me and to accomplish His work.' " Later, in John 17:4, He prayed, " 'I glorified You on the earth, having accomplished the work which You have given Me to do.' " To Jesus, doing the will of His Father was all that mattered—not applause, praise, popularity, fame, wealth, or anything else. He lived to finish God's work. That is godliness.

Application Questions:

1. How did Enoch's life exhibit godliness?

2. How did Paul's life exhibit godliness?

3. How did the psalmist's life exhibit godliness?

4. How did Christ's life exhibit godliness?

5. What definition of godliness could you put together from these examples?

GODLINESS IS GOD-CENTEREDNESS

The word "godliness" means "to be devout, to be pious." I believe that *the essence of godliness is being God-centered, or God-conscious.* A godly person is like a compass whose needle is set towards God. Though the needle may occasionally be knocked away from its center, it always returns there. In the same way, a godly person is sometimes distracted by the cares of this world, but as soon as their mind is released from these other things, it returns to God. God is the center of their life.

As the psalmist so well expressed, the essence of godliness is also that *God is enough.* The godly person can say with David, "The Lord is my shepherd, *I shall not want*" (Psalm 23:1). I heard once that when a little boy was asked what that verse meant, he replied, "It means that the Lord is my shepherd and that's all I need. Everything else is just icing on the cake." I believe that we ought to measure our godliness in terms of where we are in reference to that statement.

Is it enough to have God and God alone? More than that, is it *completely satisfying* to have God and God alone?

Jean Fletcher wrote a book called *Between Walden and the Whirlwind.* In her book, she explained how we often run around trying to meet the demands of daily life, feeling very stressed and unsatisfied with our inability to get everything done. At one point, she used the New York City Ballet Company and its former director as an illustration.

Mr. George Balanchine co-founded and directed for many years the New York City Ballet Company. He was a highly skilled and gifted man in the art of ballet who was not only the company's director, but as Fletcher noted, was their sole audience as well. What the author meant by this was that the members of the company not only respected Mr. Balanchine so highly that his word was heeded completely and never questioned, but they desired his approval so much that they danced their best for his praise alone.

Likewise, in a godly person's life, God is their sole director. We are constantly taking orders from Him and we are never in a place to question, argue, or debate His orders. We are never expected to make up our own mind about things or act according to our own desires. Proverbs 3:5-7 reminds, "Trust in the Lord with all your heart and do not lean on your own understanding. In all your ways acknowledge Him, and He will make your paths straight. Do not be wise in your own eyes; fear the Lord and turn away from evil."

II Corinthians 10:5 says it this way, "...we are taking every thought captive to the obedience of Christ." In other words, in every situation we ask, "Lord, what do You want me to do?" If God is truly our director, we must seek His direction in every area of our life and we must follow it without dispute or delay.

More than that, in the godly person's life, God is their sole audience. Whether or not anyone else is pleased, the approval of God is all that matters. The godly person may be criticized by friends, family, or colleagues, but these things have no effect if God is pleased. The God-conscious person is chiefly aware of God as his or her audience and thinks, says, and does for God's pleasure alone.

Application Questions:

1. What is the essence of godliness?

2. What are the implications of God as sole director of our life?

3. What are the implications of God as sole audience in our life?

4. How would your life be different if you lived by Proverbs 3:5-7?

HOW IS TRUE GODLINESS ATTAINED?

Understanding now what godliness is and is not, let's consider the last of our three initial questions: how can we attain true godliness? Looking back at I Timothy 4, we find this command, "...*discipline yourself* for the purpose of godliness" (4:7). The New King James Version translates this verse, "...*train yourself* to be godly." Consider three important things in this command.

First, Paul instructed us to discipline, or train, *ourselves*. Ultimately, we can discipline no one but ourselves. As teachers, spouses, or parents, we can (and should) exhort, teach, and encourage others, but we cannot *make* anyone be godly. Husbands cannot train their wives, and wives cannot train their husbands in godliness. Parents cannot train their children in godliness.

Because only God can work in the heart and only we can individually respond to that working, we are responsible to train *ourselves*. Our pastor cannot make us more godly people. The church, the elders, our Sunday school teachers—none of these people can cause an increase in our godliness. We must pursue our own growth.

Second, Paul instructed us to *gumnazo* ourselves. In different versions of the Bible, this Greek word is translated by the words "discipline," "train," and "exercise." In verse 10, Paul wrote, "For it is for this we *labor and strive…*" The word that is translated "labor" is the Greek word *kopiao* which means "to work hard, labor, be wearied." In other words, Paul is stressing the fact that our pursuit of godliness will not be easy. In fact, it will require some holy sweat.

In Colossians 4:12, Paul wrote that Epaphras was "always laboring earnestly" for the church at Colossae in his prayers. A great man of God named David Brainerd ministered to the Delaware Indians in the eighteenth century. It is said that Brainerd would sometimes go out into the woods to pray in the middle of winter. In the bitter cold, he would pray with such fervency and earnestness that he would return soaked in sweat. This man labored intensely for God.

Do we labor that intensely for godliness? Do we agonize in prayer? Do we discipline ourselves? In his book "Spiritual Disciplines for the Christian Life," Donald Whitney wrote:

> So many professing Christians are so spiritually undisciplined that they seem to have little fruit or power in their lives. I have seen men and women who discipline themselves for the purpose of excelling in their profession, but discipline themselves very little for the purpose of godliness. I have seen Christians who are faithful to the church of God who frequently demonstrate genuine enthusiasm for the things of God and who dearly love the Word of God, but trivialize their effectiveness for the kingdom of God through lack of discipline. Spiritually, they are a mile wide and an inch deep. There are no deep, time-worn channels of communing discipline

between them and God. They have dabbled in everything but disciplined themselves in nothing.

Consider the people who work hard at learning to play an instrument, knowing that it takes years to acquire the skills, who will practice hard to lower their golf score or to improve their sports performance, knowing that it takes years to become proficient, and who will discipline themselves throughout their career because they know it takes sacrifice to succeed. These same people will give up quickly when they find the spiritual disciplines do not come easily, as though becoming like Jesus is not supposed to take much effort.

The goal of godliness is not found on the surface of Christianity. It has to be dug from the depths with the tools of discipline. But for those who persevere, the treasures are more than worth the troubles. Watching a Christopher Parkening or Chet Atkins play guitar gives the impression that these guitarists were born with the instrument attached to their bodies. They have an intimacy and freedom with the guitar that makes playing look easy. Anyone who has ever tried to play realizes that the musical freedom of such masters comes from decades of disciplined practice.

Freedom through discipline is seen not only in the proficient musician, but also in the all-star short stops, expert carpenters, successful executives, well-prepared students and moms who daily manage home and family well. What is this freedom of godliness? Think again of our illustrations. For instance, a guitar virtuoso is free to play a different arrangement of Segovia, while I am not. Why? Because of his years of disciplined practice. Similarly, those who are free to quote Scripture are those who have disciplined themselves to memorize God's Word. There's a freedom from self-centeredness that is found in disciplines such as worship, service, and evangelism.

Truly, in every other area of life, we know that success rarely comes without hard work and discipline.

Mike Singletary was a linebacker for the Chicago Bears and was voted to the All-Pro team many times.

Twice he was voted the most valuable defensive player in the league. Such success in football, especially as a linebacker, might lead us to believe that Singletary was an enormous hulk of a man and an imposing presence on the football field. In fact, he was only six feet tall and weighed about two hundred pounds.

The "secret" to his success was not the size that he was born with, but the discipline that he imposed on himself. He ran plays forty or fifty times a day. He watched tapes for hours and hours. He studied his opponents' every move. He was a great football player because he dedicated himself to perfecting every aspect of his game.

My friends, if we want to become godly, we must dedicate ourselves in the same way. This is what the Scripture teaches: train yourself. The Greek word *gumnazo*, which is translated "train," literally means "to practice naked." It was used to describe the training of athletes because at that time, athletes would strip themselves of everything that could hinder their performance, including all of their clothes, before practicing or competing. The Olympic athletes of ancient Greece always competed in the nude.

I believe that this is what the writer of Hebrews had in mind when he wrote, "Therefore…*let us also lay aside every encumbrance and the sin which so easily entangles us*, and let us run with endurance the race that is set before us" (Hebrews 12:1). In other words, in order to follow Christ for a lifetime, we must remove everything that hinders us. We must be willing to put off and deny ourselves anything that does not further the goal of godliness.

In Romans 13:14, Paul exhorted, "But put on the Lord Jesus Christ, and *make no provision for the flesh in regard to its lusts.*" We may say that we want to become godly, but our true desire can be measured by our willingness to sacrifice for it. There are many things in life that are good, but not the best. If godliness is most important, then the things that are best are the only things that we will have time for.

We must each examine ourselves carefully and honestly. What distracts one person will not distract another. What hinders one person may not hinder another. As Paul said, "All things are lawful for me, but all things are not helpful. All things are lawful for me, but I will not be brought under the power of any" (I Corinthians 6:12).

If we want to grow in godliness, we must figure out what things are holding us back and then discipline ourselves to put off those things. We must also ask ourselves whether our efforts towards godliness could be characterized as *laboring and striving*, as Paul wrote in I Timothy 4:10. Do we sweat from the strain? Do we feel the pain of sacrifice?

Finally, notice that Paul's instruction to "train yourself" is in the present tense. Training ourselves for godliness is not something that is ever completed in this lifetime. It begins at salvation and continues (or *should* continue) until we reach heaven.

I read an article once about physical fitness that said when regular physical exercise is discontinued for a time, up to fifty percent of muscle tone and overall fitness is lost in just three to four weeks. As a young man, I was very physically fit because I exercised and conditioned my body for football. After college, however, I became so busy with ministry and pastoral work that exercise just fell by the wayside and, of course, the fitness that came with it. Now, that fitness is long gone.

So also, in the spiritual realm, is continued discipline necessary for continued spiritual fitness. If we want to be godly every day we must train ourselves every day. Becoming a godly person is not a one-time event; it is an on-going process.

Consider the children of Israel as an example. When God brought them out of Egypt, He could have simply swept them up and dropped them into Canaan, having already wiped out their enemies. Instead, God brought them from Egypt to Canaan through much time and many trials. They experienced plagues, forty years of wandering in the wilderness, a monotonous diet, and battles with great enemies. Nothing about their journey from slaves in Egypt to a free nation in the Promised Land was easy or quick.

Why does God deal with us in this way? We get so tired of striving, laboring, training, and struggling in life. Sometimes we cry out to God for deliverance from our trials and temptations. What we often fail to realize or remember is that God's way is always best. No matter how hard it is or long it takes, God's way is always right and always necessary.

As believers, we can be confident that whatever we experience, easy or difficult, is for our benefit. The Israelites needed to experience trials in order to grow. God was teaching them to rely on Him for their every need and to serve Him alone. If we want to grow in godliness, we must be dedicated, committed, and willing to struggle to learn the things of God.

Application Questions:

1. What are the implications of Paul's command to train ourselves for godliness?

2. What are the implications of Paul's command to train, or discipline, ourselves for godliness?

3. In light of I Corinthians 6:12, Romans 13:14, and Hebrews 12:1, what are some entangling sins in your life that you now realize you need to put off in order to pursue godliness?

4. What are some encumbrances (things that are not necessarily sin, but are hindering your progress) that you need to put off in order to pursue godliness?

5. Considering the experience of the Israelites, what are the implications of desiring and living a life of godliness?

TRUE SUCCESS GOD'S WAY

In the end, the purpose of our lives as Christians is not to become successful for our own benefit, but to become more and more like Christ for the purpose of bringing Him the glory and honor He deserves. Since Jesus Christ is our supreme example of godliness, it is only by increasing in godliness that we fulfill our highest calling in life: "For those He foreknew, He also predestined to become conformed to the image of His Son…" (Romans 8:29). Godliness is true success as God intended for us.

In light of these things, we must ask ourselves if this is what we *really* want. Do we want the kind of success—true success—that God intended for us? Do we want to stand before God in the end and find that we have laid up treasures in heaven, which last forever, or treasures on earth, which were burned up in the fire?

...each man's work will become evident; for the day will show it because it is to be revealed with fire, and the fire itself will test the quality of each man's work. If any man's work which he has built on it remains, he will receive a reward. If any man's work is burned up, he will suffer loss; but he himself will be saved, yet so as through fire. (I Corinthians 3:13-15)

Let us not be distracted by things that hinder our training for godliness. Let us throw off everything that encumbers and make every effort to pursue godliness. This is our high calling in Christ and this is true success.

Not that I have already obtained it or have already become perfect, but I press on so that I may lay hold of that for which also I was laid hold of by Christ Jesus. Brethren, I do not regard myself as having laid hold of it yet; but one thing I do: forgetting what lies behind and reaching forward to what lies ahead, *I press on toward the goal for the prize of the upward call of God in Christ Jesus.* (Philippians 3:12-14)

Application Questions:

1. What is the ultimate goal of godliness?

2. Look up the following verses on godliness. For each one, write out what application they have to what you have just learned.

a) I Timothy 2:9-10
b) I Timothy 6:3-6
c) II Peter 1:3

3. For what wrong reasons have you desired success in the past?

4. How have you pursued success in a wrong way in the past?

5. What is true success, as far as God is concerned, for His children?

6. Why are the benefits of godliness worth far more than all of the things that the world considers to be part of true success?

7. When a problem arises or a decision needs to be made, is your first thought, "What does God want me to do?" or is it, "How am I going to figure this out?"

8. Which of these do you rely most on for guidance in your life: your own experience, your own desires and opinions, the advice of other people, or the commands of God?

9. How often do you think about whether God is pleased with your thoughts, words, and actions?

10. How often are you influenced by the praise or criticism of other people?

11. What is something that you have in the past or are now working very hard to attain or accomplish (job promotion, academic grade, financial goal, etc.)?

12. Have you ever worked that hard at godliness? Why or why not?

13. Are you willing to do whatever it takes to pursue godliness? Why or why not?

14. What are some practical, definite steps that you will commit to taking to intensify your pursuit of godliness (be specific)?

15. Write out I Timothy 4:7-8. Work on memorizing these verses.

Man's
Greatest Need

WHAT DOES MAN REALLY NEED?

"If you were stranded on a deserted island with no hope of rescue, what ten items would you want to have?" This common survival challenge has no right answer, of course, because different people have different needs and different skills. It is mostly used to encourage critical thinking because it forces people to think about the most essential items for their survival.

Likewise, if we were to ask someone, "What is man's greatest need?" the answer given would depend on the person asked. A biologist or physician might answer that man's greatest need is physical: food, water, and shelter. After all, their experience demonstrates that without these things, people can quickly die. On the other hand, a psychologist might answer that man's greatest need is for fulfillment of desire or for love. In their experience, those who live without these things, though they may live physically, "die" mentally and emotionally.

Abraham Maslow, a well-known psychologist, perceived man's greatest need in this way:

> What makes people neurotic? My answer was in brief that neurosis, seen at it's core and in it's beginning, is a deficiency disease that is it born out of being deprived of certain satisfaction which I call "needs". When those needs are not satisfied, you become ill either physically or psychologically. Most of neurosis involves ungratified wishes for safety, for belongingness and identification, for close love relationships, and for respect and prestige.

Maslow's analysis fits well with that of Freud and a host of other secular psychologists who all believe that man's greatest need is purely psychological.

Another psychologist, a disciple of Sigmund Freud named Erik Erickson, broke down the human life span into eight stages. According to his theory, individuals have certain basic needs during each of these time periods. If their needs are not met during each stage, the deficiency is carried over into each later stage. These deficiencies then cause the psychological problems that a person experiences throughout life.

Some Christians agree with this assessment. A book called "Love is a Choice," written by three Christians, claims that humans have an innate, God-given need to be loved. It goes on to say that this need must be met from "cradle to grave," and if it is not met in children, they carry the scars for life. The authors use a cup as an illustration of our capacity and need for fulfillment. They say that throughout our lives, our cups are in various stages of fullness. When the cup is low, it is then that we experience problems.

Who is right? Is man's greatest need physical—food, water, and shelter? Or is psychological—to be loved and respected, to have a good self-image, to belong to a group, or to find meaning and purpose in one's life? The more people that we would ask, the more answers we would get.

There is only one answer—or Answerer, however, that is correct. Our Creator, who knows us better than we will ever know ourselves, has the only correct answer to this question. If we really want to know what man's greatest need is, we need to find out what God says about it.

Application Questions:

1. **Why do some people say that man's greatest need is physical?**

2. **Why do some people say that man's greatest need is psychological?**

3. **Why is God's answer the only correct answer?**

GOD'S ANALYSIS

Is man's greatest need physical? To answer this question from God's perspective, we need only to look at what Jesus taught in Matthew 6:25: "For this reason I say to you, do not be worried about your life, as to what you will eat or what you will drink; nor for your body, as to what you will put on." In other words, man's greatest need is *not physical.*

Is man's greatest need psychological? In an article for the *Journal of Biblical Counseling*, Dr. Edward Welch wrote:

> This category of psychological needs has entered into contemporary Christian thought without any biblical consultation. This intrusion is understandable considering the nearly universal experience of psychological need. After all, what does it feel like when a friend lets you down? Or you are unfairly criticized? Or someone manipulates you? The reactions these experiences evoke in you are seen to be manifestations of psychological needs. But no matter how

commonplace such experiences are, the needs they are said to reveal are hard to locate biblically. Page through an index of any standard theological text and what you will find is that psychological needs are absent. The only place they can be found is in the history of secular psychology...Need theories can only thrive in a context where the emphasis is on the individual rather than the community, where consumption is a way of life.

What Dr. Welch was saying in that last sentence is that if we were to ask Asians or Africans about their psychological needs, they would not even understand the question. This is because "psychological need" is largely a western phenomenon that has arisen from self-centered societies. Western intellectuals have invented the idea of psychological need by looking at human experience without the wisdom of the One who created it.

So then, what is God's perspective on man's greatest need? I believe that God's answer to this question may be found in Ephesians 1:7: "In Him we have redemption through His blood, the forgiveness of our trespasses, according to the riches of His grace." Man's greatest need, according to our Creator, is forgiveness.

Let's briefly consider three reasons why forgiveness is God's answer to man's greatest need. First, I believe that this is true because of what the Bible teaches about Christ's primary mission on earth. According to Luke 2:11, God's Son came to earth to be a Savior: "For today in the city of David there has been born for you a Savior, who is Christ the Lord."

Why do we need a Savior? We need a Savior because we need salvation from our sins. In John 1:29, John the Baptist hailed Jesus as "the Lamb of God who takes away the sin of the world!" Every one of us is born with a sin problem that only God can fix through the blood of His Son.

After the crucifixion and resurrection, Jesus gave instructions to His apostles and disciples about what they were to do after He left them: "Go therefore and make disciples of all the nations, baptizing them in the name of the Father and the Son and the Holy Spirit, teaching them to observe all that I commanded you..." (Matthew 28:19-20). Jesus commissioned His apostles to preach the forgiveness of sins because He knew that forgiveness was and is man's greatest need.

Throughout the book of Acts, in almost every recorded message of the apostles, the emphasis was on salvation through the forgiveness of sins. After hearing Peter's sermon on the day of Pentecost, the people listening cried out, "Brethren, what shall we do?" Peter's reply was this, "Repent, and each of you be baptized in the name of Jesus Christ *for the forgiveness of your sins...*" (Acts 2:37-38).

Second, I believe that man's greatest need is God's forgiveness because of what God says about the true nature of our sin. Scripture says that sin is rebellion against God. In Psalm 51:4, David wrote, "*Against You, You only, I have sinned* and done what is evil in Your sight, so that You are justified when You speak and blameless when You judge."

The Bible uses many different terms to describe sin: wickedness, rebellion, perversion, transgression, trespass, defilement, iniquity…to name a few. These terms emphasize different aspects of the horrible nature of sin, but perhaps the greatest witness to the nature of sin is its result: death and destruction. Romans 6:23 teaches, "*For the wages of sin is death*, but the free gift of God is eternal life in Christ Jesus our Lord." The death that sin brings is both physical and spiritual. Isaiah 59:2 says, "But your iniquities have made a separation between you and your God, and your sins have hidden His face from you so that He does not hear."

Third, man's greatest need is for God's forgiveness because the consequences of sin so far outweigh an abundance or deficiency of *anything* else. If a person had all of their physical and psychological needs met (theoretically speaking), it would all be worthless without God's forgiveness. While a lack of physical and psychological provisions is bearable, eternal separation from God is not. The

Bible teaches that those who do not have the forgiveness of God for their sins will spend eternity in a lake of fire, which burns with fire and brimstone. Forgiveness is indeed man's greatest need.

Application Questions:

1. What is God's analysis of man's greatest need?

2. What was Christ's primary mission on earth? How does this relate to forgiveness being man's greatest need?

3. What is the ultimate consequence of sin? How does this relate to forgiveness being man's greatest need?

4. Why is the ultimate consequence of sin unbearable? How does this relate to forgiveness being man's greatest need?

THE NATURE OF GOD'S FORGIVENESS— BY HIS GRACE AND ACCORDING TO HIS RICHES

In Ephesians 1:7, the apostle Paul provided us with some amazing truths about God's forgiveness: "In Him we have redemption through His blood, the forgiveness of our trespasses, according to the riches of His grace." In the rest of this chapter, we will study what Paul revealed about the nature of God's forgiveness in this verse.

First, forgiveness is *by the grace of God.* God's "grace" is His unmerited favor towards man. More than that, God's grace is His giving to His children the very opposite of what they deserve. As sinners, we deserve only the judgement, condemnation, and punishment of God. In other words, we deserve to spend eternity in hell.

Instead of giving us what we deserve, however, God has determined to give us the very opposite of this: forgiveness, no condemnation, and great reward. If we are His children, we have the privilege of spending eternity with Him enjoying everything that He has given us by His grace and that we did not deserve. Forgiveness is God's grace.

Second, forgiveness is *according to the riches* of God's grace. Ephesians 2:7 teaches, "so that in the ages to come He might show the *surpassing riches of His grace* in kindness toward us in Christ Jesus." Ephesians 3:8 reveals, "To me, the very least of all saints, this grace was given, to preach to the Gentiles the *unfathomable riches of Christ…*"

God's grace is according to His true riches, which are "surpassing" and "unfathomable." In fact, our finite minds cannot begin to imagine the depths of God's grace. Praise God that we can never reach its bottom, use it up, or drain it dry!

The vastness of God's grace is a wonderful thing, but the real treasure in this teaching is that Paul said that God forgives us "*according to* the riches" of God's grace. The words "according to" are very significant because they indicate that God forgives us "in keeping with" or "equal to" the riches of His grace. How significant is that? Consider this analogy.

A very poor man meets a very wealthy businessman. He begs this person for help, following him and harassing him until the wealthy man finally pulls out his checkbook and writes the poor man a check for a hundred dollars. The businessman, because he just wants to get rid of the poor man, gives to him *out of* his riches. After all, a hundred dollars to him will never be missed.

Suppose now that the outcome is different. This time, the wealthy man has great compassion on the poor man and writes him a check for a million dollars. Now, the wealthy man is giving to the poor man *according to* his riches. A million dollars is representative of the extent of the businessman's wealth, while the hundred dollars was merely a small piece of his greater wealth.

Most of us, though it might hurt a bit, could also write a check for a hundred dollars to someone in need. Very few, if any, of us could write out a check for a million dollars. Our resources simply are not that great.

God's resources, on the other hand, are infinite. When He forgives, He grants us forgiveness *according to* the riches of His grace. In other words, His infinite grace is given to us in infinite measure. Though our sins may seem infinite at times (and to our minds, they are), they are finite in God's sight and His grace covers them with abundance. We have been given grace far beyond what we require for forgiveness, for problems, and for difficulties—for all that we need.

Application Questions:

1. What is the significance of our forgiveness being by the grace of God?

2. What is the significance of our forgiveness being according to the riches of God's grace?

3. Is it possible for anyone to have too many sins for God's forgiveness to cover? Why or why not?

THE NATURE OF GOD'S FORGIVENESS— PRESENT AND COMPLETE

Third, Paul said that we "*have* redemption." The word "have" is in the present tense and means that forgiveness is a glorious reality in our lives *right now.* Forgiveness is not something that we may or may not get, or that we look forward to in the future. We have forgiveness now.

I have counseled many people who struggled with knowing whether or not they had been forgiven. I knew a man who read his Bible constantly and prayed for hours at a time. He was completely devoted to seeking God, but when I asked Him about his eternal destiny, his reply was, "All I can hope is that when I stand before God, He will forgive me."

The truth is, we do not have to wonder about whether or not we are forgiven, or hope for it to be granted us sometime in the future. The Bible says that right now we can be certain of forgiveness of sins. In Luke 19:9, Jesus said to Zaccheus, "*Today* salvation has come to this house…" If we have asked Christ for forgiveness, acknowledging Him as Savior and Lord, we may be certain that our greatest need is already met.

Fourth, Paul taught that we have *forgiveness* of our sins. What does the Bible mean when it talks about "forgiveness"? The Greek word *aphiemi* is the word that is most often translated "forgive" in the New Testament and means "to send away, remit, cancel, or erase."

I heard of a woman who claimed to be a Christian but admitted that she had not talked with another woman for a long time. In fact, she would not allow this other woman into her home and avoided her at all cost. Another Christian said to this first woman that she ought to forgive the other woman, to which she replied, "I've forgiven her, but I don't want anything to do with her."

While that may be some people's idea of forgiveness, praise God that His forgiveness is not like that! Consider what the Scripture tells us about God's forgiveness:

As far as the east is from the west, so far has He removed our transgressions from us. (Psalm 103:12)

"Come now, and let us reason together," says the Lord, "Though your sins are as scarlet, they will be as white as snow; though they are red like crimson, they will be like wool." (Isaiah 1:18)

"I have wiped out your transgression like a thick cloud and your sins like a heavy mist..." (Isaiah 44:22)

He will again have compassion on us; He will tread our iniquities under foot. Yes, You will cast all their sins into the depths of the sea. (Micah 7:19)

"And their sins and their lawless deeds I will remember no more." (Hebrews 10:17)

...having forgiven us all of our transgressions, having canceled out the certificate of debt consisting of decrees against us, which was hostile to us... (Colossians 2:13-14)

ABSOLUTE FORGIVENESS!

What incredible pictures God has given us of His forgiveness! We owed Him a tremendous debt, but He cancelled that debt and no longer holds us responsible. Every sin has been wiped away and removed so far from us and from God that it can never be recovered.

A little girl came home from school after her first day of school and said to her mother, "Today in school my teacher wrote some things on a blackboard. Then she took out something and she wiped those words off the blackboard. What happened to those words, when she wiped them off?" Her mother replied, "Well, honey, they just disappeared." "Yeah, mommy," said the still confused little girl, "but where did they disappear to?" After going back and forth a few more times, her mother finally said, "Honey, you are just going to have to trust me that those words are gone and they don't exist anywhere anymore."

Thank the Lord that when He forgives us, our sins do not exist anywhere anymore either. God has promised to never bring them up against us again. Romans 8:33-34 says, "Who will bring a charge against God's elect? God is the one who justifies…" If we are justified by God, the Supreme Judge, then we are justified indeed. No one can ever bring a charge against us or hold us accountable. We have been given complete, absolute, eternal forgiveness.

Fifth, we have been granted forgiveness of "our *trespasses*." "Trespasses" is one of the many words that the Bible uses to describe sin, but what I want us to notice is that this word is plural. We have been forgiven of *all* our sin, not just some, many, or most. God's forgiveness includes the sins of our youth and old age, sins of thought and words, sins of choices we made and actions we did. *All has been forgiven.*

In I Corinthians 6:9-10, Paul described the kind of sinners that some of the Corinthian believers used to be: fornicators, idolaters, adulterers, homosexuals, thieves, covetous, drunkards, revilers, and swindlers. After listing all of these horrible sins, Paul reminded them of the good news of the gospel, "Such were some of you; but *you were washed, but you were sanctified, but you were justified in the name of the Lord Jesus Christ* and in the Spirit of our God" (6:11).

Whatever sins we have committed, or will commit, God can wipe out. If we come to Him as He has ordained, we can have *all* of our sins forgiven—no matter how heinous, no matter how many. Just as the floodwaters covered the whole earth and rose above the highest mountains (Genesis 7:19-20), so God has completely covered our sins. As the hymn writer truly said, "Grace, grace, God's grace, grace that is greater than all our sin!"

Application Questions:

1. Read Psalm 85:2, Mark 2:5, and I John 2:12. How do these verses confirm the truth that our forgiveness is a present reality?

2. Pick one of the verses that illustrate God forgiveness from the list of six given. Write out the verse. Think about and explain what this word picture tells us about how God forgives.

3. How is the flood a good illustration of the completeness of God's forgiveness—all sins, no matter how numerous or heinous?

THE NATURE OF GOD'S FORGIVENESS— THROUGH THE BLOOD OF CHRIST

Sixth, Paul taught that we have forgiveness of our sins in *Christ and through His blood*, "In Him, we have redemption through His blood…" Contrary to what some people believe, forgiveness of sins does not come by a life of sacrifice or denial. It does not come through good works, baptism, church attendance, Bible reading, or prayer.

While all of these things are important to the Christian life, they are not the means through which our sins are forgiven. According to the Word of God, forgiveness of sins comes only through Jesus Christ. "Therefore let it be known to you, brethren, that *through Him* forgiveness of sins is proclaimed to you" (Acts 13:38).

Further, this forgiveness is through *Christ's blood*. In other words, not by Christ's teaching, example, or life do we find forgiveness, but we have forgiveness by His blood. Some time ago, I was in Rome and visited a place called the Scarlet Sanctum. This place is considered to be, by tradition, the stairs that Jesus walked up on His way to the crucifixion. I watched as people visiting the site bowed down and kissed the steps where they believed His blood once lay.

Apparently, these people believed that there was some merit or grace granted to them through contact with the literal blood of Christ. In fact, some people believe a similar thing in regard to communion. The wine or grape juice taken in communion is believed, in some churches, to be miraculously transformed into the literal blood of Christ and the bread into His literal body by the blessing of the priest.

This, however, is not what Paul was indicating when he said that we have forgiveness by the blood of Christ. The words "His blood" remind us that Christ took our place when He died on the cross and it is only by His death that God forgives sinners. Paul taught, "He made Him who knew no sin to be sin on our behalf, so that we might become the righteousness of God in Him" (II Corinthians 5:21). And Peter wrote, "...and He Himself bore our sins in His body on the cross, so that we might die to sin and live to righteousness, for by His wounds you were healed" (I Peter 2:24).

Christ bore on Himself all the wrath of God and paid the penalty in full for our sins. "For Christ also died for sins *once for all*, the just for the unjust, so that He might bring us to God..." (I Peter 3:18). For those of us who are in Christ Jesus, "there is now no condemnation" (Romans 8:1). That is why Paul said, "For I determined to know nothing among you except Jesus Christ, and *Him crucified*" (I Corinthians 2:2). Man's greatest need, forgiveness, comes only by Christ, through His blood.

Application Questions:

1. **What do Acts 13:38 and I Corinthians 2:2 tell us about the means through which we can have forgiveness?**

2. **What do I Peter 2:24 and I Peter 3:18 tell us about the significance of Christ's blood for the forgiveness of sins?**

3. **Read Hebrews 9:22. Why was Christ's death necessary for the forgiveness of sins?**

THE NATURE OF GOD'S FORGIVENESS—FOR ALL WHO BELIEVE

Finally, notice that Paul wrote, "In Him we have redemption...the forgiveness of *our* trespasses..." Who was Paul including in "we" and "our"? He was certainly not referring to all people. If we look back at the beginning of this letter to the Ephesians, we find that Paul addressed his letter: "To the saints who are at Ephesus and who are faithful in Christ Jesus" (Ephesians 1:1).

The words "saints...who are faithful in Christ Jesus" indicate that this letter was and is addressed solely to people who have been united to Christ by faith. These are people who have relied on Christ alone for their salvation. Paul described these people further in the next few verses. The "we" of verse seven are those people who were "chosen...in Him before the foundation of the world" (1:4). Who is "chosen"? We know that we have been chosen if we trust in Christ alone.

The "we" of verse seven are those people who were "predestined…to adoption as sons through Jesus Christ to Himself, according to the kind intention of His will" (1:5). Who is "adopted"? We know that we have been adopted if we trust in Christ alone. Consider the words of this hymn:

Nor silver nor gold hath obtained my redemption,
Nor riches of earth could have saved my poor soul.
The blood of the cross is my only foundation,
The death of my Savior now maketh me whole.

Nor silver nor gold have obtained my redemption,
The guilt on my conscious too heavy had grown.
The blood of the cross is my only foundation,
The depth of my Savior could only atone.

Nor silver nor gold hath obtained my redemption,
The holy commandment forbade me draw near.
The blood of the cross is my only foundation,
The death of my Savior removeth my fear.

Nor silver nor gold hath obtained my redemption,
The way into heaven could not thus be bought.
The blood of the cross is my only foundation,
The death of my Savior hath wrought.

I am redeemed, but not with silver,
I am bought, but not with gold.
Bought with a price, the blood of Jesus,
Precious price of love untold.

Who, then, has forgiveness? Any person who can say that they know they are redeemed in Christ, though His blood, according to the riches of His grace, has forgiveness of their sins. And if that is true of us, we ought to be shouting for joy and praising God because our greatest need has been met!

Down through the ages, people have lived lives of great sacrifice for Christ. Hebrews 11:35-38 describes some of the difficulties that have been endured for Christ's sake: torture, imprisonment, mocking, scourging, stoning, sawing in two, temptation, death by sword, poverty, affliction, and homelessness. Yet these men and women, "having gained approval through their faith," had great hope because of their forgiveness—because their greatest need had been met.

Yes, it is nice to have our physical and psychological desires satisfied, but we do not have to be devastated or destroyed if they are not. In fact, it is quite possible (and actually commanded) for us to be content, regardless of what physical or psychological desires of ours remain unfulfilled.

Application Questions:

1. **What did Paul say were the characteristics of those who have forgiveness (Ephesians 1:1-5)?**

2. **Can you say with confidence that you are one whose sins have been forgiven? Why or why not?**

AN INVITATION TO HAVE YOUR GREATEST NEED MET

If anyone does not yet know that they are forgiven because they do not yet know Christ, I urge you to change that right now. Think about the words of Augustus Toplady's great hymn about our Lord Jesus Christ, called "Rock of Ages":

Rock of ages, cleft for me, Let me hide myself in Thee;
Let the water and the blood, From Thy wounded side which flowed;
Be of sin the double-cure, Save from wrath and make me pure.

Not the labors of my hands, Can fulfill Thy law's demands;
Could my zeal no respite know, Could my tears forever flow,
All for sin could not atone; Thou must save, and Thou alone.

Nothing in my hand I bring, Simply to the cross I cling;
Naked, come to Thee for dress; Helpless, look to Thee for grace;
Foul, I to the fountain fly; Wash me, Savior, or I die.

If you come before the Lamb of God with a spirit of repentance and humility, acknowledging your need for forgiveness and your inability to do anything for yourself, He has promised to hear you and to answer your prayer for forgiveness. Then you also can be among those who say with confidence, "In Him we have redemption through His blood, the forgiveness of our trespasses, according to the riches of His grace." Hallelujah!

Application Questions:

1. Read the parable of the rich man and Lazarus in Luke 16:19-31.

a) According to the world's analysis (physical or psychological needs being greatest) who had their needs met, the rich man or Lazarus?

b) Did the satisfaction of the rich man's needs on earth have any consequence or value to him in eternity?

c) What did the rich man recognize as man's greatest need in verse 30?

d) Sadly, the rich man in this parable recognized his greatest need when it was too late; however, it's not yet too late for you. Have you repented and asked God for forgiveness of your sins?

2. What implications does the truth about God's forgiveness being by His grace have for your life? (Consider Romans 3:23-28)

3. What implications does the truth about God's forgiveness being according to His riches have for your life? (Consider Matthew 18:21-35)

4. What implications does the truth about God's forgiveness being a present reality have for your life? (Consider Romans 6:12-18)

5. What implications does the truth about God's forgiveness being complete have for your life? (Consider Romans 5:17-6:11)

6. What implications does the truth about God's forgiveness being through the blood of Christ have for your life? (Consider Acts 4:12)

7. What implications does the truth about God's forgiveness being for all who believe have for your life? (Consider Acts 2:37-39)

✠ ✠ ✠ ✠ ✠ ✠ ✠ ✠ ✠ ✠